Foreword

It's an honour to introduce this book to you on behalf of the Rainbow Trust, the infinitely imaginative and effective charity that works with children, and the families of children, with life threatening illnesses.

Nothing, it seems, can adequately prepare us for the big things in life - when they hit us, that is, for the first time. It's true of the joyous things like falling in love or having a child, and it's even more true, somehow, of the painful things, especially the bitter pain of loss.

Grief can throw us into a loneliness that is often unbearable; a state of bewilderment and despair in which any step forward seems out of the question. It is then that the knowledge that other people have trodden this hard path before, and have not only survived, but have come to relish life again, can be a beacon of true consolation.

This anthology is a collection of such beacons. It's like a procession of little candles lit and held by other people, past and present, who have lived through this particular darkness and who understand what it's like and, what's more, how to deal with it.

It's a book of wisdom certainly, and of comfort and even humour, but most of all, and most importantly, it's a book of hope.

Joanna Trollope

Introduction

In memory of all those we love and see no longer

This anthology has been collected over a number of years. It brings together under one cover many pieces that are known and loved. I would like to thank all those who have contributed and also those who have given so generously of their advice: Tuggy Delap and Rowena Beaumont who with our publisher Tony Pooles of A3 Litho Limited have pulled the threads together.

I have tried to meet the copyright requirements and trace authors. Sadly this has proved impossible in some cases, where it has I hope that I may be forgiven. The proceeds go to Rainbow Trust.

Janet Glover

Published by Lady Glover 1997

Printed by A3 Litho Ltd. Farnham

ISBN 0953156109

Acknowledgements

We are so grateful to the publishers, writer's agents and authors for the copyright permission to reprint the following extracts:-

Peter Frazer & Dunlop group for 'From quiet homes and first beginnings,' by Hilaire Belloc; Celestial Arts, P.O. Box 7123 Berkley CA 94707 excerpt from 'Love is an attitude' copyright 1970 Walter Rinder; Rupert Crew Ltd. and Dame Barbara Cartland for 'The Light of Love.' Rupert Crew Ltd. for 'An Angel in Disguise,' 'The Purpose,' and 'Be True' by Patience Strong (world copyright reserved by the Literary Trustee of Patience Strong); John Murray Publishers Ltd. for 'The Master Shipwright' by Ronald A Hopwood; Oxford University Press for 'Aedh wishes for the cloths of Heaven' W B Yeats; A P Watt Ltd. on behalf of National Trust for 'Four Feet' by Rudyard Kipling; Times Newspaper Ltd. for 'A day in the life of Bernadette Cleary' by Sue Fox published in The Sunday Times Magazine 15 September 1996; R S Thomas for 'The Bright Field;' Lifetime Books, Inc. for 'The Greatest Salesman in the World' by Og Mandino copyright 1968 new edition 1996; Faber and Faber Ltd for 'Scaffolding' from 'Death of a Naturalist' by Seamus Heaney; Mr. George Sassoon for 'Everyone Sang' by Seigfried Sassoon; Wharncliffe Publishing Ltd. for 'Tide's Ending' from 'B.B. A Celebration'; and Jonathan Cape Ltd. for The Complete Poems of WH Davies and the executors of the Estate of WH Davies.

There must be a beginning of any great matter, but the continuing unto the end until it be thoroughly finished yields the true glory.

Sir Francis Drake

The Velveteen Rabbit

'How can I become real?'
the little velvet rabbit asked
the old rocking horse.

'It's something that happens
to you when someone loves you,
for a long time, really loves
you.'

'Does it hurt?'

'Sometimes,' answered the
rocking horse, 'but when you
are real you don't mind being
hurt.

It doesn't happen all at
once, you slowly Become. It
takes a long time, and it does
not often happen to people who
break easily, or have sharp
edges.

By the time you are real
your velvet will be worn out
and loved off, and you will
look really shabby, but these
things don't matter at all
because once you are real you
can't be ugly, except to people
who don't know how to love.'

Margery Williams

One thing I know, life can never die,
Translucent, splendid, flaming like the sun,
Only our bodies wither and deny
The life-force when our strength is done.

Let me transmit this wonderful fire,
Even a little through my heart and mind,
Bringing the perfect love we all desire
To those who seek, yet blindly cannot find.

Barbara Cartland
from The Light of Love

Do not stand at my grave and weep.
I am not there - I do not sleep,
I am a thousand winds that blow,
I am the softly falling snow,
I am the gentle rains that fall,
I am the fields of ripening grain.
I am in the morning hush,
I am in the graceful rush
Of beautiful birds in circling flight,
I am the starshine of the night.
I am in the flowers that bloom,
I am in a quiet room.
I am in the birds that sing,
I am in each lovely thing.
Do not stand at my grave and cry -
I did not die ...

There is always music amongst the trees in the garden but
our hearts must be very quiet to hear it.

A Friend

Is one to whom one may
pour out all the contents of
ones heart, chaff and grain
together, knowing that the
gentlest of hands will
take it, sift it, keep what
is worth keeping and with a
breath of kindness
throw away the rest.

When he shall die,
Take him and cut him out in little stars
And he will make the face of heaven so fine
That all the world will be in love with the night
And pay no worship to the garish sun.

William Shakespeare

Light and Shade by turn, but Love always.

A sundial at Newton Valence

Had I the heavens' embroidered cloths,
Enwrought with golden and silver light,
The blue and the dim and the dark cloths
Of night and light and the half light,
I would spread the cloths under your feet:
But I, being poor, have only my dreams;
I have spread my dreams under your feet:
Tread softly because you tread on my dreams.

WB Yeats

There is not a person anywhere who has not something within his being of value to someone else; something to give or something to share.

Lorraine Snikler

When you get what you want
in your struggle for self,
And the world makes you king for a day;
Just go to the mirror and look at yourself,
And see what that man has to say.

For it isn't your father or mother or wife,
Whose judgement upon you must pass;
The fellow whose verdict
counts most in your life,
Is the one staring back from the glass.

You may fool the whole world
down the pathway of years,
And get pats on the back as you pass;
But your final reward
will be heartache and tears,
If you've cheated that man in the glass.

There is a tide in the affairs of men,
Which, taken at the flood, leads us on to fortune;
Omitted, all the voyage of their life
Is bound in shallows and in miseries.
On such a full sea are we now afloat;
And we must take the current when it serves,
Or lose our ventures.

William Shakespeare

A drop of rain maketh a hole in the stone, not by violence, but by oft falling.

The Salutation of the Dawn

Look well to this day! For it is life,
The very life of life.
For yesterday is but a dream
And tomorrow is only a vision:
But today well lived
Makes every yesterday a dream of happiness
And every tomorrow a vision of hope -
Look well therefore to this day
Such is the salutation of the dawn.

The Sanskrit

"Old Men forget!" Aye it may well be so:
But youth remembers all the magic spun
and woven in the warm fraternal glow
of your companionship. Your day is done?
It is not true. You know you left behind
a memory of courage which the years
can but increase. And we, your heirs, will find
that in good truth there's nothing here for tears.

So be it. This your legacy to youth -
to make the best of all your days
and finally to recognise the truth
and you have shown us, silhouetted, stark,
that though we loved the sunlight's summer rays
we need not fear the coming of the dark.

Stanley of Alderley

If you cannot find a sunny side to life then polish up the dark side.

"A Mother holds her children's hands for a short while, but their hearts she holds forever."

❖

Speak to us of Children.

And he said:
Your children are not your children.
They are the sons and daughters of Life's longing for itself.
They come through you but not from you,
And though they are with you, yet they belong not to you.

You may give them your love but not your thoughts,
For they have their own thoughts.
You may house their bodies but not their souls,
For their souls dwell in the house of tomorrow,
which you cannot visit, not even in your dreams.
You may strive to be like them, but seek not to make them like you.
For life goes not backward nor tarries with yesterday.
You are the bows from which your children as living arrows are sent forth.

Kahlil Gibran

❖

How odd that children, when they paint,
Show art mature and finished skill,
While seasoned artists make a feint
Of being little children still.

You have to do your own growing, no matter how tall your grandfather was.

"A grandmother is a lady who has no children of her own, so she likes other people's children. A grandfather is a man grandmother. He goes for walks with the boys and they talk about fishing and tractors. Grandmothers don't have to do anything but be there. They are old so they shouldn't play hard or run. They should never say 'Hurry up.' Usually they are fat, but not too fat to tie children's shoes. They wear glasses and funny underwear, and they can take their teeth and gums off. They don't have to be smart, only answer questions like why dogs hate cats and why God isn't married. They don't talk baby-talk like visitors. When they read to us they don't skip bits, or mind if it is the same story over again. Everyone should have one, especially if you don't have television, because grandmothers are the only grown-ups who have time."

Quoted by an eight year old

Prayer for a Grandchild

Let no-one hurry her, Lord
Give her the rare, the incomparable gift of time,
Days to dream, dragonfly days, days when the kingfisher
Suddenly opens for her a window on wonder.
Let no-one chivvy her, Lord; let her meander
Lark-happy through childhood, by fern-curled streams
Fringed butter-yellow with kingcups; by secret ways
That paws have worn through the wild;
Give her cuckoo-loud days and the owl's cry by night.
Dear lord, give her the rainbows;
Show her a nest filled with sky-blue promises;
Scoop up the sounding oceans for her in a shell.
Let her keep her dreams.
So that she will always turn her face to the light;
Live merrily, love well;
Hold out ungloved hands to flower and child;
Be easy with animals; come to terms with time.
Lord let her keep her dreams:
Let her riches be remembered happy days.

Margaret Rhodes

Scaffolding

Masons when they start upon a building,
Are careful to test out the scaffolding.

Make sure the planks won't slip at busy points,
Secure all ladders, tighten bolted joints.

And yet all this comes down when the job's done
Showing off walls of sure and solid stone.

So if, my dear, there sometimes seem to be
Old bridges breaking between you and me,

Never fear. We may let the scaffolds fall
Confident that we have built our wall.

Seamus Heaney

God has not promised skies always blue,
Flower-strewn pathways all our lives through;
God has not promised sun without rain,
Joy without sorrow, peace without pain.
God has not promised we shall not bear
Many a burden, many a care.
He has not told us we shall not know
Toil and temptation, trouble and woe.

But God has promised strength for the day,
Rest for the labour, light for the way,
Grace for the trials, help from above,
Unfailing sympathy, undying love.

Death is part of the future for everyone. It is the last post of this life and the reveille of the next. Death is the end of our present life, it is the parting from loved ones, it is the setting out into the unknown. We overcome death by accepting it as the will of a loving God, by finding Him in it. Death, like birth, is only a transformation, another birth. When we die we shall change our state, that is all. And in faith in God, it is as easy and natural as going to sleep here and waking up there.

from 'Journey for a Soul'

❖

I will greet this day with love in my heart. And how will I do this? Henceforth will I look on all things with love and I will be born again. I will love the sun for it warms my bones; yet I will love the rain for it cleanses my spirit. I will love the light for it shows me the way; yet I will love the darkness for it shows me the stars. I will welcome happiness for it enlarges my heart; yet I will endure sadness for it opens my soul. I will acknowledge rewards for they are my due; yet I will welcome obstacles for they are my challenge.

Og Mandino

Not how did he die?
But how did he live?
Not what did he gain?
But what did he give?
These are the units to measure the worth
Of this man as a man regardless of birth.
Not what was his station?
But had he a heart?
How did he play his God-given part?
Was he at hand with a word of good cheer
To bring back a smile or banish a fear?
Not what was his church or what was his creed?
But had he befriended those really in need?
Not how did the formal obituary run?
But how many grieved when his life's work was done?

I always think that we all live, spiritually, by what others have given us in the significant hours of our life. These significant hours do not announce themselves as coming, but arrive unexpectedly. Nor do they make a great show of themselves; they pass almost unperceived. Often, indeed, their significance comes home to us first as we look back, just as the beauty of a piece of music or a landscape often strikes us first in our recollection of it. Much that has become our own in gentleness, modesty, kindness, willingness to forgive, in veracity, loyalty, resignation under suffering, we owe to people in whom we have seen or experienced these virtues at work, sometimes in a great matter, sometimes in a small. A thought which had become an act sprang into us like a spark, and lit a new flame within us..

If we had before us those who having thus been a blessing to us, and could tell them how it came about, they would be amazed to learn what passed over from their life into ours.

Albert Schweitzer

... something in you dies when you bear the unbearable. And it is only in that dark night of the soul that you are prepared to see as God sees and to love as God loves.

Never once - since the world began
Has the sun ever once stopped shining,
His face very often we could not see,
And we grumbled at his inconstancy;
But the clouds were really to blame, not he,
For behind them, he was shining.

And so - behind life's darkest clouds,
God's love is always shining.
We veil it at times with our faithless fears,
And darken our sight with our foolish tears,
But in time the atmosphere always clears,
For his love is always shining.

On an Autumn day,
I took up a handful of grain
And let it slip slowly through my fingers.
And I said to myself:
"This is what it is all about.
There is no longer any room for pretence.
At harvest time the essence is revealed.
The straw and the chaff are set aside.
They have done their job.
The grain alone matters - sacks of pure gold."

So it is when a person dies.
The essence of that person is revealed.
At the moment of death, a person's character stands out.
Happy for the person who has forged it well over the years.
Then it will not be the great achievements that will matter:
Not how much money or possessions a person has amassed.
These, like the straw and chaff, will be left behind.
It is what he has made of himself that will matter.

Death can take away from us what we have,
But it cannot rob us of who we are.
We are children of our heavenly Father,
And co-heirs with Christ to the Kingdom of Heaven.

They who are near me do not know that you are nearer to me than they are.
They who speak to me do not know that my heart is full with your unspoken words.
They who crowd in my path do not know that I am walking alone with you.
They who love me do not know that their love brings you
to my heart.

Tagore

I set my rainbow in the sky and it shall be the sign of the covenant between me and the earth.

Genesis 9:13

.... And God Created Mothers

When the good Lord was creating Mothers, he was into his sixth day of overtime when an angel appeared and said, "You are doing a lot of fiddling around on this one." And the Lord said, "Have you read the specification on this order? She has to be completely washable, but not plastic ... have one hundred and eighty movable parts - all replaceable ... run on black coffee and leftovers ... have a lap that disappears when she stands up ... a kiss that can cure anything from a broken leg to a disappointed love affair ... and six pairs of hands."

The angel shook her head slowly and said, "Six pairs of hands? No way."

"It's not the hands that are causing me problems," said the Lord. "It's the three pairs of eyes that mothers have to have." "That's on the standard model?" asked the angel. The Lord nodded. "One pair that sees through doors when she asks, 'What are you children doing in there?' when she already knows. Another in the back of her head that see what she shouldn't but what she has to know. And, of course, the ones in front that can look at a child when he gets himself into trouble and say 'I understand and I love you' without so much as uttering a word."

"Lord," said the angel, touching him gently, "Go to bed. Tomorrow is another day" "I can't I'm so close now. Already I have one who heals herself when she is sick, can feed a family of six on one pound of mince, and can get a nine-year old to have a bath," said the Lord The angel circled the model very slowly. "It's too soft," she sighed. "But tough," said the Lord, excitedly. "You cannot imagine what this mother can do and endure."

"Can it think?" - "Not only think but it can reason and compromise," said the Creator. Finally the angel bent over and ran her finger across the cheek. "There's a leak," she said. "It's not a leak," replied the Lord, "It's a tear." "What's it for?" "It's for joy, sadness, disappointment, pain, loneliness and pride." "You're a genius!" said the angel. The Lord looked sombre - "I didn't put it there."

Every blade of grass has its Angel that bends over it and whispers, "Grow, grow."

The Talmund

A smile costs nothing, but gives much.
It enriches them who receive,
Without making poorer them who give.
It takes but a moment,
Yet the memory of it may last forever.
A smile creates happiness in the home,
Fosters goodwill in business,
And is the sign of friendship.
It brings rest to the weary,
Cheer to the discouraged,
Sunshine to the sad,
And is nature's best antidote to trouble.
Yet a smile cannot be bought, begged,
borrowed or stolen;
For it is something of no value to anyone,
Unless it is given away.
Some people are too tired to give you a smile.
Give them one of yours.
No one needs a smile so much as
He who has none to give.

Age is a quality of mind;
If you have left your dreams behind,
If hope is cold,
If you no longer look ahead,
If your ambitious fires are dead,
Then you are old.

But if in life you take the best,
And if in life you keep the jest,
If love you hold;
No matter how the years go by,
No matter how the birthdays fly,
You are not old.

The tree of life my soul hath seen,
Laden with fruit, and always green:
  The trees of nature fruitless be
Compared with Christ the apple tree.

For happiness I long have sought,
And pleasure dearly I have bought:
  I missed of all; but now I see
'Tis found in Christ the apple tree.

❖

My soul, sit thou a patient looker on;
Judge not the play before the play is done;
Her plot hath many changes; everyday
Speaks a new scene; the last act crowns the play.

Francis Quarles

❖

In time the curtain edges will grow light.

❖

One never gets a second chance to make a first impression.

Instead of seeing the rug pulled from under us, we can learn to dance on a shifting carpet.

Light looked down and beheld Darkness,
"Thither will I go," said Light.
Peace looked down and beheld War,
"Thither will I go," said Peace.
Love looked down and beheld Hatred,
"Thither will I go," said Love.
So came Light, and shone;
So came Peace, and gave rest;
So came Love, and brought Life
And the Word was made Flesh, and dwelt among us.

Laurence Housman

To laugh often and love much, to win the respect of intelligent persons and the affection of children; to earn the approbation of honest critics and to endure the betrayal of false friends; to appreciate beauty; to find the best in others; to give one's self; to leave the world a bit better, whether by a healthy child, a garden patch or a redeemed social condition; to have played and laughed with enthusiasm and sung with exultation; to know even one life has breathed easier because you have lived, this is to have succeeded.

Ralph Waldo Emerson

In so much as love grows in you so in you beauty grows.
For love is the beauty of the soul.

St Augustine

We are as great as the dreams that we dream,
As great as the love we bear,
As great as the values we redeem,
And the happiness we share.
We are as great as the truth we speak,
As great as the help we give,
As great as the destiny we seek,
As great as the life we live.

American Indian Wedding Prayer

Now you will feel no rain
For each of you will be shelter to the other.

Now you will feel no cold
For each of you will be warmth to the other.

Now you will feel no loneliness
For each of you will be companionship to the other.

Now you are two persons
But there is only one Life between you.

Go now to your dwelling place
To enter into the days of your life together.

Prayer of Columba

Almighty Father, Son and Holy Ghost.
Eternal ever-blessed gracious God,
To me, the least of saints, to me, allow
That I may keep a door in Paradise:
That I may keep even the smallest door.
The furthest door, the darkest coldest door,
The door that is least used, the stiffest door.
If so it be but in thine house. O God!
If so it be that I can see Thy Glory
Even afar, and hear Thy Voice, O God!
And know that I am with Thee -
Thee, O God.

W Muir

Cast your bread upon the waters and it will come back buttered.

Lord, thou knowest, better than I know myself, that I am growing older and will soon be old.

Keep me from getting talkative, and particularly from the fatal habit of thinking I must say something on every occasion.

Release me from the craving to try and straighten out everybody's affairs.

Make me thoughtful but not moody, helpful but not bossy.

With my vast store of wisdom it seems a pity not to use it all! But thou knowest, Lord, that I want a few friends at the end.

Keep my mind from the endless recital of details.

Give me wings to get to the point.

Seal my lips on many aches and pains; they are increasing and my love of rehearsing them is becoming sweeter as the years go by.

Teach me the glorious lesson that occasionally it is possible that I may be mistaken.

Keep me reasonably sweet.

I do not want to be a saint - some of them are hard to live with - but a sour old woman is one of the works of the devil.

' What is this world? A dream within a dream - as we grow older, each step is an awakening. The youth awakes, as he thinks, from childhood - the full-grown man despises the pursuits of youth as visionary - the old man looks on manhood as a feverish dream. The grave, the last sleep? - No; it is the last and final awakening.

Walter Scott

There is no limit to what a man can do if he doesn't mind who gets the credit.

The Bright Field

I have seen the sun breakthrough
to illuminate a small field
for a while, and gone my way
and forgotten it. But that was the pearl
of great price, the one field that had
the treasure in it. I realize now
that I must give all that I have
to possess it. Life is not hurrying

on to a receding future, nor hankering after
an imagined past. It is the turning
aside like Moses to the miracle
of the lit bush, to a brightness
that seemed as transitory as your youth
once, but is the eternity that awaits you.

RS Thomas

An Angel in Disguise

A song - a line of poetry - a sermon or a flower - will seem to hold some special meaning in the darkest hour... An unexpected gift - a friendly deed from one unknown - A smile - a sympathetic word - a little kindness shown ... It's strange how just a simple thing can help us on our way, and strengthen us and hearten us throughout the weary day ... And so through human agency God's purpose is unrolled; He works in deep mysterious ways his secrets to unfold ... In every good and lovely thing some hidden meaning lies ... The stranger at your door may be an angel in disguise.

Patience Strong

Shoot for the moon - even if you miss you will land
among the stars.

Life Thoughts

May all your tomorrows hold the special happiness, that's wished for you today. No matter what our yesterdays have been, tomorrow may be different. As long as we have life, the fires of hope will not die out. With the thought of a new day, the flame that seems dead leaps forward, and the sparks once more fly upward to spur us on.
Tomorrow may hold your fate ... Tomorrow may hold your victory .... The great joy of expectation ... The wonderment of an unknown realm ... The splendour of the vast fortune lies in the eternal tomorrow ... The day for which Life is worth Living.

The Word

What is the real good?
I asked in musing mood,
Order - said the law court;
Knowledge - said the school;
Truth - said the wise man;
Pleasure - said the fool;
Love - said the maiden;
Beauty - said the page;
Freedom - said the dreamer;
Home - said the sage;
Fame - said the soldier;
Equity - said the seer.

Spake my heart full sadly:
The answer is not here.
Then within my bosom
Softly this I heard:
Each heart holds the secret,
Kindness is the Word.

If we really know how to go to sleep we will know how to die ... To go knowingly through the threshold from the object world to the objectless world is to forget all the residues of the person and so be open to a new dimension of life. It is an offering back to life all the expressions that life gave us temporarily. Then what remains is original consciousness.

Jean Klein

Tide's Ending

See where those leaning poplars stand
Along the far sea wall?
That is the outpost of the land,
There is the end of all,
Geese in skein, and the sound again
Of their clanging bugles blending,
Samphire sent, and a great content
In the place I call Tide's Ending.

Follow the sheep track's winding thread,
Draw deep the down wind blowing,
All the world is still and dead,
Only the tide is flowing,
Curlews call from the dim sea wall,
We'll take what the gods are sending,
The first gulls come, the flight's begun
In the place I call Tide's Ending

Mark yon wheel of the Bar Point light
Uneasy in the gloaming,
Timid spark in the world of night,
Guide for a curlew's laying
Whistle of wings and ghostly things
beyond all comprehending,
Tang of the sea,
And the soul set free
In the place I call Tide's Ending.

B B

One of the best erasers in the world is a good night's sleep.

Let your hook be always cast; in the pool where you least expect it, there will be a fish.

You can't live on hope, but it should be on the Menu.

Pray for me as I shall for thee: that we may love and laugh again when we meet merrily in heaven.

Sir Thomas Moore
His last letter to his daughter

"Life is eternal and love immortal, and death is only an horizon, and an horizon is nothing save the limit of our sight."

Our birth is but a sleep and a forgetting;
The soul that rises with us, our life's star
Hath elsewhere its setting,
And cometh from afar;
Not in an entire forgetfulness,
And not in utter nakedness,
But trailing clouds of glory do we come
From God, who is our home.

William Wordsworth

The Rose Beyond the Wall

Near shady wall a rose once grew,
Budded and blossomed in God's free light,
Watered and fed by morning dew,
Shedding it's sweetness day and night.

As it grew and blossomed fair and tall,
Slowly rising to loftier height,
It came to a crevice in the wall,
Through which there shone a beam of light.

Onward it crept with added strength,
With never a thought of fear or pride;
It followed the light through the crevice-length
And unfolded itself on the other side.

The light, the dew, the broadening view,
Were found the same as they were before;
And it lost itself in beauties new,
Breathing it's fragrance more and more.

Shall claim of death cause us to grieve
And make our courage faint or fall?
Nay, let us faith and hope receive;
The rose still grows beyond the wall.

Scattering fragrance far and wide,
Just as it did in the days of yore,
Just as it did on the other side,
Just as it will for evermore.

AL Frink

❖

The Fruit of The Spirit is:-

Love
Joy
Peace
Patience
Kindness
Goodness
Faithfulness
Gentleness
Self control

Against these things there is no law.

Galatians 5:2.2

A man can only do what he can do. But if he does that each day he can sleep at night and do it again the next day.

Albert Schweitzer

People travel to wonder at the height of the mountains, at the huge waves of the sea, at the long courses of rivers, at the vast compass of the ocean, at the circular motion of the stars; and they pass by themselves without wondering.

St Augustine

The winds of grace blow all the time.
All we need to do is set our sails.

Ramakrishna

Love is silence when your words would hurt,
Patience when your neighbour's curt;
It's deafness when the scandal flows;
It's thoughtfulness for another's woes;
It's promptness when stern duty calls.
It's courage when misfortune falls.

Fly away, fly away bird to your native home,
You have leapt free of the cage
Your wings are flung back in the wind of God
Leave behind the stagnant and marshy waters,
Hurry, hurry, hurry, O bird, to the source of life!

Rumi

"Pilgrim, when your ship long moored in harbour, gives you the illusion of being a house; when your ship begins to put down roots in the stagnant waters by the quay; put out to sea! Save your boat's journeying soul and your own pilgrim soul, cost what it may."

Helda Camara

"For life, with all it yields of joy
and woe, and hope and fear,
is just one chance of the prize
of learning love."

Robert Browning

Crossing The Bar

Sunset and evening star,
    And one clear call for me!
And may there be no moaning of the bar,
    When I put out to sea.

But such a tide as moving seems asleep,
    Too full for sound and foam,
When that which drew from out the boundless deep
    Turns again home.

Twilight and evening bell,
    And after that the dark!
And may there be no sadness of farewell,
    When I embark;

For tho' from out our bourne of Time and Place
    The flood may bear me far,
I hope to see my Pilot face to face
    When I have crost the bar.

Lord Tennyson

You cannot travel on the path before you have become the Path itself.

Guatama Buddha

Silently, one by one, in the infinite meadows of heaven, bloomed the lovely stars, the forget-me-nots of the angels.

Longfellow

Any fool can count the seeds in one apple - but who can count the apples in one seed?

I saw stretching right across in front of us the high white shoulders of the Himalayas. They seemed to stoop over the plain, lifting the blue hem of their foothills out of the smoke and dust of the flat lands. Cold, clean and aloof, they disdained the dirt and toil below. 'One day,' I thought, 'one day soon, I must go there,' and my eyes followed the distant peaks and ridges.

Miles Smeeton

❖

The daffodils are paid for by the January snow.
Without the shadow of suffering we would not know
the light of joy.

❖

Ships are safe in the harbour but that's not what they're meant for.

❖

Some men see things as they are and ask why?
I dream of things that never were and ask why not?

John F Kennedy

❖

Never measure the height of a mountain till you have reached the top. Then you will see how low it was.

Dag Hammarskjold

The life of man on earth, my lord, in comparison with the vast stretches of time about which we know nothing, seems to me to resemble the flight of a sparrow, who enters through a window in the great hall warmed by a blazing fire laid in the centre of it, where you feast with your councillors and liegemen, while outside the tempests and snows of winter rage. And the bird swiftly sweeps through the great hall and goes out the other side, and after this brief respite from winter, he goes back into winter and is lost to your eyes. Such is the brief life of man, of which we know neither what goes before nor what comes after.

Venerable Bede

Everyone Sang

Everyone suddenly burst out singing;
And I was filled with such delight
As prisoned birds must find in freedom,
Winging wildly across the white
Orchards and dark-green fields; on; on;
and out of sight.

Everyone's voice was suddenly lifted,
And beauty came like the setting sun:
My heart was shaken with tears and horror
Drifted away ... O, but everyone
Was a bird; and the song was wordless;
the singing will never be done.

Siegfried Sassoon

The woods would be very silent if no birds sang but those which sang the best.

Henry Van Dyke

How Great the Yield from a Fertile Field

The farmer ploughs through the fields of green
And the blade of the plough is sharp and keen,
But the seed must be sown to bring forth grain,
For nothing is born without suffering and pain-
And God never ploughs in the soul of man
Without intention and purpose and plan,
So whenever you feel the plough's sharp blade.
Let not your heart be sorely afraid.
For, like the farmer, God chooses a field
From which He expects an excellent yield -
So rejoice though your heart is broken in two,
God seeks to bring forth a rich harvest in you.

I am in the Wind that caresses you;
I am in the Sun that shines upon you;
I am in the Rain that cools you and makes you grow;
I am in the Stones under your feet and in the tranquillity of the Pool.

Rex Riant

I asked God for all things that I might enjoy life.
God gave me life that I might enjoy all things.

Death is not the extinguishing of the light,
but the putting out of the lamp because
the dawn has come.

Tagore

Dig a hole in your garden of thoughts. Into it put all your disillusions, disappointments, regrets, worries, troubles, doubts and fears, and - forget. Cover well with earth of fruitfulness, water it from the well of content. Sow on top again the seeds of hope, courage, strength, patience, and love. Then, when the time of gathering comes, may your harvest be a rich and plentiful one.

The Clock of Life is wound but once,
and no man has the power
to tell just when the hands will stop;
at late or early hour.
Now is the only time you own,
Live! Toil with a will!
Place no faith in tomorrow;
For the clock may then be still.

Love is not changed by death, so nothing is lost
and all in the end is harvested.

Edith Sitwell

Bring us, O Lord God, at our last awakening into the house and gate of heaven, to enter into that gate and dwell in that house, where there shall be no darkness nor dazzling but one equal light; no noise nor silence, but one equal music; no fears nor hopes, but one equal possession; no ends nor beginnings, but one equal eternity; in the habitations of thy glory and dominion, world without end.

John Donne

"All shall be well and thou shalt see it thyself
that all manner of things shall be well."

Julian of Norwich

For what is it to die but to stand naked in the wind and to melt into the sun?
And what is it to cease breathing, but to free the breath from its restless tides, that it may rise and expand and seek God unencumbered?
Only when you drink from the river of silence shall you indeed sing.
And when you have reached the mountain top, then you shall begin to climb.
And when the earth shall claim your limbs, then shall you truly dance.

Kahlil Gibran

❖

"No medicine is more valuable,
none more efficacious, none
better suited to the cure
of all our temporal ills
than a friend to whom
we may turn for consolation in time
of trouble and with whom
we may share our happiness in times of joy."

St Aelred of Rievaulx

I will make you brooches and toys for
your delight
Of bird-song at morning and
starshine at night.
I will make a palace fit for you
and me
Of green days in forests and
blue days at sea.

Robert Louis Stevenson

To everything there is a season,
And a time to every purpose under the heaven;
A time to be born and a time to die;
A time to plant, and a time to pluck up that which is planted;
A time to kill, and a time to heal;
A time to break down, and a time to build up;
A time to weep, and a time to laugh;
A time to mourn, and a time to dance;
A time to cast away stones, and a time to gather stones together;
A time to embrace, and a time to refrain from embracing;
A time to get, and a time to lose;
A time to keep, and a time to cast away;
A time to rend and a time to sew;
A time to keep silence, and a time to speak;
A time to love, and a time to hate;
A time of war and a time of peace...
Wherefore I perceive that there is nothing better,
than that a man should rejoice in his own works;
for that is his portion; for who shall bring him
to see what shall be after him?

Ecclesiastes III

Lord, I have Time,
I have plenty of time,
All the time that you give me,
The years of my life,
The days of my years,
The hours of my days,
They are all mine.
Mine to fill quietly and calmly;
But to fill completely, up to the brim.

The value of life lies not in the length of days but in the use of them.

Montaigne

If God be for us, who can be against us?

A Lamartine

Close now thine eyes and rest secure;
Thy soul is safe enough, thy body sure;
He that loves thee, He that keeps
And guards thee, never slumbers, never sleeps.
The smiling conscience in a sleeping breast
Has only peace, has only rest;
The music and the mirth of Kings
Are all but dischords, when she sings:
Then close thine eyes and rest secure,
No sleep so sweet as thine, no rest so sure.

Francis Quarles

❖

Let naught disturb thee,
Naught fright thee ever.
All things are passing.
God changeth never.

St Teresa

I asked God to help me find love.
He told me, You are love.
I asked God to help me find purpose.
He told me, You are purpose.
I asked God to help me find truth.
He told me, You are truth,
And when you find Me,
Your questions will end.

Walter Rinder

If God shuts a door, he opens a window.

The Purpose

When the sun has set in some far dim hour, and the world is tired and old; when the last faint note of the song dies out, and the final tale is told; when the tools and weapons are laid aside, with the chisel and the pen and brush ... God's voice will ring through the halls of space, from the depths of a timeless hush.
He will speak of deep and eternal things, far beyond our human ken - The secret working of unseen powers in the destinies of men ... And hearing, we shall be satisfied, to know that it was not vain - the rage of grief, and the heart's red wounds, the desiring, and the pain.
When the soul has flung off its last despair, with its hungers and its fears - having gazed deep down in wells of Truth for a million lonely years ... It will know the purpose behind it all; it will know and understand, why love has its price, and why sorrow must be - in the things that He has planned.

Patience Strong

Kneelers

Discarded hassocks, soon to go these
Which lie neglected by the vestry door;
Yet each has borne the weight of praying knees
And heard the desperate longings of the poor.

How happy if these ancient hassocks here
Could pass to our new kneelers all they know
Of penitence, of worship and of prayer
And tears which God alone has seen to flow.

E K W

The God of Heaven so join you now, that you may be glad of one another all your lives; and when He which has joined you shall separate you, may He again establish you with an assurance that He has but borrowed one of you for a time, to make both more perfect in the Resurrection.

Lord, make me an instrument of
your peace,
Where there is hatred, let me
sow love,
Where there is injury, pardon,
Where there is doubt, faith,
Where there is despair, hope,
Where there is darkness, light,
and where there is sadness, joy.
O, Divine Master, grant that I
may not so much seek to be
consoled, as to console,
To be understood, as to understand,
To be loved as to love.
For it is in giving that we receive.
It is in pardoning that we are
pardoned,
And it is in dying that we are
born to eternal life.

St Francis of Assisi

Prayer was not invented. It was born
in the first sigh, the first joy, the first
sorrow of the human heart.

A Lamartine

He said

I long to take your load,
I want to bear your burdens too
But this you must remember
This one thing you must know,
I cannot take your burden
Until you let it go.

A Dream

One night I had a dream,

I dreamed I was walking along the beach with the Lord,
and across the sky flashed scenes from my life.

For each scene, I noticed two sets of footprints in the sand;
One belonged to me, the other to the Lord.

When the last scene of my life flashed before me,
I looked back at the footprints in the sand.

I noticed that many times along the path
There was only one set of prints.

I noticed that it happened at the very lowest
and saddest times in my life,
and I questioned the Lord about it:

'Lord, You said that once I decided to follow You,
You would walk with me all the way.

But I have noticed that during
the most troublesome times in my life,
there is only one set of footprints.

I don't understand why in times when I need you most,
You would leave me.'

The Lord replied: 'My precious , precious child,
I love you and I would never, never leave you
during your times of trial and suffering.

When you see only one set of footprints -
It was then that I carried you.'

God be in my head, and in my understanding;
God be in my eyes and in my looking;
God be in my mouth and in my speaking;
God be in my heart and in my thinking;
God be at my end, and at my departing.

Positive Count

Count your blessings instead of your crosses;
Count your gains instead of your losses;
Count your joys instead of your woes;
Count your friends instead of your foes;.
Count your courage instead of your fears;
Count your laughs instead of your tears;
Count your full years instead of your lean;
Count your kind deeds instead of your mean;
Count your health instead of your wealth;
Count on God instead of yourself.

Flattery rarely hurts a man unless he inhales.

God gave us the grass but he doesn't cut it for us!

Sometimes the worst thing
God can do for you is to
grant you your wishes

Happiness is to be found among life's common things. It is not great wealth, great learning, great genius or great power; it is not these things that make the possessors happy. It is health, friendship, love at home; it is the voices of children, it is sunshine. It is the blessings that are commonest not those that are the rarest.

At Day's End

Is anybody happier because you passed this way?
Does anybody remember that you spoke to him today?
The day is almost over, and its toiling time is through,
Is there anyone to utter now a kindly word of you?

Can you say tonight, in parting with the day that's slipping fast,
That you helped a single brother of the man that you passed?
Is a single heart rejoicing over what you did or said?
Does the man whose hopes where fading, now with courage look ahead?

Did you use the day, or lose it? Was it well or sorely spent?
Did you leave a trail of kindness or a scar of discontent?
As you close your eyes in slumber, do you think that God will say,
"You have earned one more tomorrow by the work you did today"?

Face the sun and the shadows will fall behind you.

When many rejoice together,
The joy of each is richer,
They warm themselves at
Each other's flame.

St Augustine

From quiet homes and first beginnings
Out to the undiscovered ends,
There's nothing worth the wear of winning,
But laughter and the love of friends.

Hilaire Belloc

Quiet minds cannot be perplexed or frightened, but go on in fortune or misfortune at their own private pace, like a clock during a thunderstorm.

Take time to THINK
    it is the source of power.
Take time to PLAY
    it is the secret of perpetual youth.
Take time to READ
    it is the fountain of wisdom.
Take time to PRAY
    it is the greatest power on earth.
Take time to LOVE and BE LOVED
    it is God's greatest gift
Take time to BE FRIENDLY
    it is the road to happiness.
Take time to LAUGH
    it is the music of the soul.
Take time to GIVE
    it is too short a day to be selfish.
Take time to WORK
    it is the price of success.
Take time to be CHARITABLE
    it is the key to heaven.

People wrapped up in themselves make very small parcels.

Thy friend has a friend, and thy friend's friend has a friend:
Be discreet!

The Talmund

We have not realised Religion in its perfection, even as we have not realised God. Religion of our conception, being thus imperfect, is subject to a process of evolution. And if all faiths outlined by men are imperfect, the question of comparative merit does not arise.

Even as a tree has a single trunk, but many branches and leaves, so there is one true and perfect Religion, but it becomes many, as it passes through the human medium. The one Religion is beyond all speech. Imperfect men put into such language as they can command, and their words are interpreted by other men equally imperfect. Whose interpretation is held to be the right one? Everybody is right from his own standpoint, but it is not possible that everybody is wrong. Hence the necessity of tolerance, which does not mean indifference to one's own faith, but a more intelligent and purer love for it. Tolerance gives us spiritual insight, which is as far from fanaticism as the North Pole from the South. True knowledge of Religion breaks down the barriers between faith and faith.

Mahatma Ghandi

If love must go, then let it gently pass
Let no vain, proud, or bitter word be spoken,
But with the natural summer in the grass,
Let love depart, yet leave the heart unbroken.
All seasons change. Believe me, you shall feel,
Beneath white solitude, the slow wounds mending
Till spring's old promise, once more green and real,
Startles your heart with word of winter's ending.

RH Grenville

The greatest pleasure I know, is to do a good action by
stealth and to have it found out by accident.

Charles Lamb

The Master Shipwright

The ships in Chailey Dockyard lay crippled as they could be,
Rigging and masts and timbers, and in no-wise fit for sea;
And some, tho' new from the cradle, seemed only built to fail,
And none might to windward in the teeth of a winter gale.

So the shipwrights came to Chailey to succour the ships therein,
For this is the craftsman's honour, to prove what his skill may win;
But gravely they spake and graver, as they saw the halt and lame:
'We must send for the Master Shipwright', so the Master Shipwright came.

And no man saw His coming, but His presence was noon-tide clear,
In the work of the toiling shipwrights, who worked with exceeding cheer.
He wrought no mighty magic, but He taught them day by day
To use the gifts He gave them, for that is the Master's way.

New faith he gave to the shipwrights, that shone in the craftsman's skill,
New hope to the ships they tended, the hope no wounds may kill.
But a message more than either, to toil for the Master's sake;
And the shipwrights learned the message, that the Master Shipwright spake.

For it wedded love to labour, and that's why their labour lives,
And who shall measure the giving, when the Master Shipwright gives?
Till the shipyard sang with service, as ship by ship was gained
To carry whole her topsails, nor fear that a mast be strained.

So the craft from Chailey Dockyard go forth from the building slips
('Twas ever the oaks from Sussex that fashioned the stoutest ships),
To speed with summer breezes, or fight with a searching wind,
To join in the Master's service, in the service of mankind.

They hail and cheer in passing, they signal great and small,
For the mark of the Master Shipwright is on them and through them all;
They carry the shipwrights' message, on a thousand new-won keels,
That men know of the healing wherein the Master heals.

Rear Admiral Ronald A Hopwood CB

At the very darkest point of night, one must believe in
the dawn ...

I found God in the morning.
We just sat and talked.
I kept him near me everywhere I walked.
I called God at noontime, a heart filled with despair.
I felt his quiet presence, I knew He was there.
We met again at sunset,
The waneing of the day,
I had made him happy, I had lived his way.
Then at bedtime I knelt
Silently in prayer.
Again his gentle presence I felt:
"Someone does care".

Teach us, good Lord, to serve thee as thou deservest; to give and not to count the cost; to fight and not to heed the wounds; to toil and not to seek for rest; to labour and not to ask for any reward save that of knowing that we do thy will.

'Follow the makers instructions and all will be well.'

Notice outside a church

"O Lord, thou knowest how busy I must be this day: If I forget thee, do not Thou forget me."

❖

Horses she loved, laughter and the sun,
All beauty, wide spaces and the open air.
The trust of all dumb living things she won.
And never knew the luck too good to share.

And though she may not ride this way again,
Her joyous spirit rides onward yet,
Freed from all chance of weariness or pain,
Forbidding us to mourn or to forget.

Patricia Mitchell

Upon a day, a woman who had died
Came to the Gates of Heaven, and saw outside
St Peter, writing in his Book of Gold,
The dreary lies that everybody told.

The woman waited, with averted head,
Until St Peter looked at her and said:
"Tell me, O Traveller, with the pilgrim pack,
What loves and hates you carry on your back."

"I love my garden, Sir," the woman said.
"I loved my flowers, and now that I am dead
I only ask that someone will be kind
To that dear garden I must leave behind."

The key was turned, the Gates were opened wide.
St Peter and woman walked inside;
And there, within the sunshine of the throne,
She saw the little garden she had grown.

Reginald Arkell

The sun may be clouded, yet ever the sun
Will sweep on its course till the Cycle is run.
And when into chaos the system is hurled
Again shall the Builder reshape a new world.

Your path may be clouded, uncertain your goal:
Move on - for your orbit is fixed to your soul.
And though it may head into darkness of night.
The touch of the Builder shall give it new light.

You were, you will be! Know this while you are:
Your spirit has travelled both long and afar.
It came from the Source, to the Source it returns -
The Spark which was lighted eternally burns

It slept in a jewel. It leapt in a wave.
It roamed in the forest. It rose from the grave.
It took on strange garbs for long eons of years
And now in the soul of yourself it appears.

From body to body your spirit speeds on
It seeks a new form when the old one has gone
And the form that it finds is the fabric you wrought
On the loom of the Mind from the fibre of Thought.
As dew is drawn upwards, in rain to descend
Your thoughts drift away and in Destiny blend.
You cannot escape them, for petty or great,
Or evil or noble, they fashion your Fate.

Somewhere on some great planet, sometime and somehow
Your life will reflect your thoughts of your Now.
My Law is unerring, no blood can atone -
The structure you built you will live in - alone.
From cycle to cycle, through time and through space
Your lives with your longings will ever keep pace.
And all that you ask for, all that you desire,
Must come at your bidding, as flame out of fire.

Once list' to that Voice and all tumult is done -
Your life is the Life of the Infinite One.
In the hurrying race you are conscious of pause
With love for the Purpose, and love for the Cause.

You are your own Devil, you are your own God;
You have fashioned the paths your footsteps have trod.
And no-one can save you from Error or Sin
Until you have hark'd to the Spirit within.

A Maori prayer

Four Feet

I have done mostly what most men do
And pushed it out of my mind;
But I can't forget if I wanted to
Four feet trotting behind.
Day after day, the whole day through
Wherever my road inclined,
Four feet said "I'm coming with you"
And trotted along behind.
Now I must go by some other road-
Which I shall never find-
Somewhere that does not carry the sound
Of four feet trotting behind.

Rudyard Kipling

It is hard
To forget
To apologise
To save money
To be unselfish
To avoid mistakes
To begin all over again
To make the best of things
To keep your temper
To think first and act afterwards
To keep on keeping on
To shoulder blame
To be charitable
To admit error
To take advice
To forgive -
But it pays!

"Courage is the art of being the only one who knows you're scared to death".

The evening comes, the field is still;
The trickle of the thirsty mill,
Unheard all day, ascends again;
Deserted is the new reaped grain,
Silent the sheaves the ringing wain,
The reapers cry, the dog's alarms,
All housed within the sleeping farms!
The business of the day is done,
The last belated gleaner gone,
And from the thyme upon the height,
And from the elder blossom white,
And pale dog-roses in the hedge,
And from the mint plant in the sedge,
In puffs and balm the night air blows
The perfume which the day forgoes
And on the pure horizon far,
See, pulsing with the first-born star,
The liquid sky above the hill!
The evening comes, the field is still.

Matthew Arnold
from Bacchanalia

I would be true for there are those who trust me;
I would be pure, for there are those who care,
I would be strong, for there is much to suffer,
I would be brave, for there is much to dare;
I would be friend of all, the foe, the friendless:
I would be giving, and forget the gift;
I would be humble, for I know my weakness;
I would look up, and laugh, and love, and live.

Some day when you're feeling important;
Some day when your ego's in bloom;
Some day when you take it for granted
You're the best qualified in the room;
Some day when you feel that your going
Would leave an unfillable hole
Just follow these simple instructions
And see how they humble you soul.
Take a bucket and fill it with water,
Put your hand in it up to the wrist,
Pull it out, and the hole that's remaining
Is a measure of how you'll be missed.
You can splash all you wish when you enter,
You may stir up the water galore,
But stop, and you'll find that in no time
It looks just the same as before.

The moral of this is quite simple,
To do just the best that you can;
Be proud of yourself, but remember
There is no indispensable man.

And yet there's a Man up in Heaven
Without whom each man lives in vain;
Though we can dispense with all others
He's the one indispensable Man.
He came into the world to save sinners
And no other man could do this,
For only Christ Jesus can take us
From Earth to Heaven's glorious bliss
We can do without this one or that one,
It's quite easy to soon fill their place;
But to do without Christ means disaster,
With a life gone to ruin and waste.

The moral of this is quite simple
Take Christ as your Saviour and Friend
Then you'll see him one day up in Heaven
Where joys know no measure nor end.

The best mirror is an old friend.

George Herbert

Overheard in an Orchard

Said the Robin to the Sparrow,
"I would really like to know
Why these restless human beings
Rush about and worry so?"

Said the Sparrow to the Robin
"Friend I think that it must be
That they have no Heavenly Father
Such as cares for you and me."

Be True

Be true to the best that is in you - hold on to the good and the real; be true to the hope that you cherished and follow your highest ideal.

Be true to your own intuition and trust it to lead you aright; when darkness descends round your pathway keep straight, and look up to the light.

Be true to your high aspirations; be true to the vows that you made; be true to yourself, and your conscience and face any man, unafraid.

And when the last conflict is ended, the last battle over and won, a voice out of heaven will greet you with, well done, good servant, well done.

Patience Strong

I said to the man who stood at the gate of the year: 'Give me a light that I may tread safely into the unknown.'

And he replied: 'Go out into the darkness and put your hand into the hand of God. That shall be to you better than a light and safer than a known way.'

M Louise Haskins

Leisure

What is this life if, full of care,
We have no time to stand and stare.

No time to stand beneath the boughs
And stare as long as sheep and cows.

No time to see when woods we pass,
Where squirrels hide their nuts in grass.

No time to see, in broad daylight,
Streams full of stars, like skies at night.

No time to turn at Beauty's glance,
And watch her feet, how they can dance.

No time to wait till her mouth can
Enrich that smile her eyes began.

A poor life this if, full of care,
We have no time to stand and stare.

WH Davies

A man should never be ashamed to own he has been in the wrong, which is but saying that he is wiser today than yesterday.

Pope

Slow me down, Lord! Ease the pounding of my heart by the quieting of my mind. Steady my hurried pace with a vision of the eternal reach of time. Give me, amidst the confusion of my day, the calmness of the everlasting hills. Break the tensions of my nerves and muscles with the soothing music of the singing streams that live in my memory.

Help me know the magical, restoring power of sleep. Teach me the art of taking minute vacations.

... Of slowing down to look at a flower, to chat with a friend, to pat a dog, to read a few lines from a good book. Remind me each day of the fable of the hare and tortoise that I may know that the race is not always to the swift; that there is more to life than measuring its speed.

Let me look upward into the branches of the towering oak and know that it grew great and strong because it grew slowly and well. Slow me down, Lord and inspire me to send my roots deep into the soil of life's enduring values that I may grow towards the stars of my great destiny ...

Holborn

If all the good people were clever,
And all the clever people were good,
The world would be better than ever
We thought it possibly could.
But alas it is seldom or never
That the two hit it off as they should
For the good are so kind to the clever
And the clever so rude to the good!

Search not for a good man's pedigree.

Ex Ore Infantium

LITTLE JESUS, wast Thou shy
Once, and just as small as I?
And what did it feel like to be
Out of Heaven and just like me?
Didst Thou sometimes think of there,
And ask where all the angels were?
I should think that I would cry
For my house all made of sky;
I would look about the air,
And wonder where my angels were;
And at waking 'twould distress me -
Not an angel there to dress me!
Hadst Thou ever any toys,
Like us little girls and boys?
And didst Thou play in Heaven with all
The angels that were not too tall,
With stars for marbles? Did the things
Play *Can you see me?* through their wings?
And did Thy mother let Thee spoil
Thy robes with playing on our soil?
How nice to have them always new
In Heaven, because 'twas quite clean blue!

Didst Thou kneel at night to pray,
And didst Thou join Thy hands this way?
And did They tire sometimes, being young,
And make the prayers seem very long?
And dost Thou like it best that we
Should join our hands to pray to Thee?
I used to think before I knew,
The prayer not said unless we do.
And did Thy Mother at the night
Kiss Thee and fold the clothes in right?
And didst Thou feel quite good in bed,
Kissed, and sweet, and Thy prayers said?

Thou canst not have forgotten all
That it feels like to be so small:
And Thou knowest I cannot pray
To Thee in my father's way
When Thou wast so little, say,
Couldst Thou talk Thy Father's way? -

continued/

So, a little Child, come down
And hear a child's tongue like Thy own;
Take me by the hand and walk,
And listen to my baby-talk.
To Thy Father show my prayer
(He will look, Thou art so fair)
And say: 'O Father, I, Thy Son,
Bring the prayer of a little one;'
And He will smile, that children's tongue
Has not changed since Thou wast young!

Francis Thompson

Do not let us fear things too much, for we
often suffer more from the things we fear
than from those which really come to
pass... Rejoice to think that after having
recovered yourself in the midst of interior
pain and difficulty, you will be able to help others
in their turn. No one can help except
he who has suffered. . . .

Abbe de Tourville

Do not envy unduly the good fortune of others:
There are many who would like your status.

Rather light a candle than complain about the darkness.

If there be righteousness in the heart,
    There will be beauty in the character.
If there is beauty in the character,
    There will be harmony in the home.
If there is harmony in the home,
    There will be order in the nation.
When there is order in the nation,
    There will be peace in the world.

Perhaps, if we could see.
    The splendour of the land
    To which our loved are called from you and me
    We'd understand.
Perhaps, if we could hear
    The welcome they receive
    From old familiar voices - all so dear -
    We would not grieve.
Perhaps, if we could know
    The reason why they went
    We'd smile - and wipe away the tears that flow
    And wait content.

The place whence comes each happy inspiration ...
Where love serenely dwells ... and hope is born ...
Where strivings cease .. and strife is barred the door.
Where confidence is bred .. and the eloquence of silence understood.
A place where plans are made and journeys start,
    where journeys end in happy welcomings.

Where dwells that peace so eagerly desired by all ...
    and mutual trust survives whate're befall.

Where laughter is not very far away, and truth is reverenced.
Where friends drop in to share our joys or woes,
    and absent friends are ever in our thoughts.

God give you such a home.

If you've any task to do
Let me whisper, friend to you... Do it.

If you've anything to say,
True and needed, yea or nay... Say it.

If you've anything to love,
As a blessing from above... Love it.

If you've anything to give,
That another's joy may live... Give it.

If some hollow creed you doubt,
Though the world hoot and shout... Doubt it.

If you know what torch to light
Guiding others through the night... Light it.

If you've any debt to pay,
Rest you neither night nor day... Pay it.

If you've any joy to hold,
Next your heart, lest it get cold... Hold it.

If you've any grief to meet,
At the loving Father's feet... Meet it.

If you're given light to see
What a child of God should be.. See it.

Whether life be bright or drear,
There's a message sweet and clear,
Whispered down to every ear... Hear it.

Dean of Chichester

DEATH is nothing at all . . I have only slipped away
into the next room . . . I am I and you are you . . .
whatever we were to each other that we are still. Call me
by my old familiar name, speak to me in the easy way
which you always used. Put no difference into your tone;
wear no false air of solemnity or sorrow. Laugh as we
always laughed at the little jokes we enjoyed together.
Play, smile, think of me, pray for me. Let my name be ever
the household word that it always was. Let it be spoken
without an effort, without the ghost of a shadow on it.
Life means all that it ever meant. It is the same as it ever
was; there is absolutely unbroken continuity. What is death
but a negligible accident? Why should I be out of your mind
because I am out of your sight? I am but waiting for you, for
an interval, somewhere very near just around the corner.
All is well.

Henry Scott Holland

I stand upon a sea shore, a ship spreads her white sails to the morning breeze, and heads across the blue ocean. She is an object of beauty and strength, and I stand and watch her until at length she hangs like a speck of white cloud on the horizon just where the sea and the sky meet to mingle with each other. At my side someone says, "There! She's gone."

Gone where? Gone from my sight - that is all. She is just as large in mast and spar and hull as when we sailed close by, and just as able to bear her living freight to the place of destination. Her diminished size is in my vision alone. At the moment when someone says "There! She's gone," other eyes watching her coming and other voices take up the shout, "Here she comes!"

And that is dying.

Bishop Brent

You touched my life
And turned my life around.
It seems when I found you
It was me I really found.
You opened my eyes
And now my soul can see
Our moments may be over,
Of just you here with me.

Love lived on beyond Goodbye
And truth of us will never die.
Our spirits will shine
Long after we've gone,
And so our love lives on.

There was so much
I didn't understand
When you brought me here
Far from where we all began.
The changes you made
To my life will never end.
I'll look across the distance
And know I have a friend.

Love lives on beyond Goodbye
The truth of us will never die.
Our spirits will shine
Long after we've gone,
And so our love lives on.

And so our love lives on.

God, grant me the serenity to accept the things I cannot change, courage to change the things I can, and the wisdom to know the difference.

The Dusk is Down

"The dusk is down on the river meadows,
The moon is climbing above the fir,
The lane is crowded with creeping shadows,
The gorse is only a distant blur,
The last of the light is almost gone;
  But hark! They're running!
      They're running on!

The count of the years is steadily growing,
The Old give way to the eager Young;
Far on the hill is the horn still blowing,
Far on the steep are the hounds still strung,
Good men follow the good men gone,
  And hark! They're running!
    They're running on!"

The life that I have is
 all that I have,
And the life that I have is yours.
The love that I have
 of the life that I have
Is yours and yours and yours.

A sleep I shall have,
 a rest I shall have
Yet death will be but a pause,
For the peace of my years
 in the long green grass
Will be yours and yours and yours.

For Violette Szabo

Each player must accept the cards life deals him or her. But once they are in hand, he or she alone must decide how to play the cards in order to win the game.

Voltaire

❖

If you think you are beaten, you are;
If you think you dare not, you don't;
If you'd like to win but you think you can't
It's almost certain you won't.

If you think you'll lose, you've lost;
For out of the world we find,
Success begins with a fellow's will;
It's all in the state of mind.

If you think you're outclassed, you are;
You've got to think high to rise;
You've got to be sure of yourself before
You can ever win the prize.

Life's battles don't always go,
To the stronger or faster man;
But sooner or later the man who wins,
Is the one who THINKS he can.

Happiness is like a butterfly. The more you chase it, the more it eludes you. Then you turn your mind to other things and it comes and sits silently on your shoulder.

If I should die and leave you here a while
Be not like others sore, undone, who keep
Long visits by the silent dust and weep.
For my sake turn again to life and smile,
Nerving thy heart and trembling hand to do
Something to comfort other hearts than thine.
Complete these dear unfinished tasks of mine,
And I, perchance, may comfort you.

Finally Brethren

whatsoever things are true,
whatsoever things are honest,
whatsoever things are just,
whatsoever things are pure,
whatsoever things are lovely,
whatsoever things are of
good report; if there be any
virtue, and if there be any
praise, think on these things.

Philippians 4

So, if the flight of a bird is so beautiful
So strange and so sweet,
How more beautiful yet must be the flight of the soul towards God.
What a glory and a sweeping on the wind
Of the wings of the spirit towards light.

Dorothea Eastwood
from Flight

Then Almitra spoke again and said, And what of Marriage, master?
And he answered saying:
You were born together, and together you shall be for evermore.
You shall be together when the white wings of death scatter your days.
Aye, you shall be together even in the silent memory of God.
But let there be spaces in your togetherness.
And let the winds of the heavens dance between you.
Love one another, but make not a bond of love:
Let it rather be a moving sea between the shores of your souls.
Fill each other's cup but drink not from one cup.
Give one another of your bread but eat not from the same loaf.
Sing and dance together and be joyous, but let each one of you be alone.
Even as the strings of a lute are alone though they quiver with the same music.
Give your hearts, but not into each other's keeping.
For only the hand of Life can contain your hearts.
And stand together yet not too near together:
For the pillars of the temple stand apart,
And the oak tree and the cypress grow not in each other's shadow.

Kahlil Gibran

After a while you learn
The subtle difference
Between holding a hand
And chaining a soul.
And you learn
That love doesn't mean leaning
And company doesn't mean security.
And you begin to learn
That kisses aren't contracts
And presents aren't promises.
And you begin to accept your defeats
With your head up and your eyes ahead
With the grace of a woman or a man
Not with the grief of a child.
And you learn to build all your roads on today
Because tomorrow's ground is
Too uncertain for plans
And futures have a way of falling down
In mid-flight.
After a while you learn
That even the sunshine burns if you ask too much.
So you plant your own garden
And decorate your own soul
Instead of waiting for someone to bring you flowers
And you learn
That you can really endure
That you are really strong
And you really do have worth.
And you learn ...
And you learn ...
With every failure
You learn.

For while the tired waves, vainly breaking,
Seem here no painful inch to gain,
Far back through creeks and inlets making,
Comes, silent, flooding in, the main.

And not by eastern windows only,
When daylight comes, comes in the light,
In front the sun climbs slow, how slowly,
But westward, look, the land is bright.

Arthur Hugh Clough
from Say Not The Struggle
Naught Availeth

❖

'True love is drowned by no billows of
mischance: true love fears no thunder
bolts of fate: true love abides immortal,
firm, unchangeable. To have loved once
is to love for aye.'

Montrose

Trouble is a tunnel through which we must pass, not a
brick wall against which we have to break our heads.

Believe in yourself but keep it a secret.

I'll lend you, for a while a child of mine, God said.
For you to cherish while he lives and mourn for when he's dead.
It may be months, or even years, an hour or two, or three.
But will you 'til I call him come look after him for me?
He'll bring you his love to gladden you, and should his stay be brief,
You'll have the sweetest memory as solace for your grief.
I cannot promise he will stay, since all from Earth return,
But love's a lesson taught below, I want this child to learn.
I've looked the wide world over in search for teachers true,
And from the throngs that crowd life's land
At last I've chosen you!
Now will you give him all your love.
Nor think your labour vain,
Nor turn against Me when I come to take him home again?

~ ❖ ~

Quotes from Rainbow's Children

"Andrew was on the phone, Mum. He's fed up with being dead and he's coming home for tea."

Emily saw heaven as being up in the sky. She looked up one day in the garden and asked "which cloud does Andrew live on?"

Emily

JIM: (in wheelchair) What are you crying for?
BROTHER: I'm crying because you're leaving us
JIM: Don't be silly . . . you know the big bedroom we share?
When I go you can have it all to yourself
BROTHER: (visibly brightening) Oh yeah . . . What about your music centre then?
JIM: (appalled) You're not having that! I'm taking it with me. . .

All of a sudden the little boy said "We seem to have forgotten our brother already." The others said "No we haven't, he's on the sand making sand castles with us."

An Old Gaelic Blessing

May the road rise up to meet you:
May the sun shine always on your face:
May the wind be always at your back:
May the rains fall gently on your fields and gardens:
And until we meet again, may God keep you
in the hollow of His Hand.

Conclusion

'Unless you have experienced being with a child at the moment of death, there is a paralysing fearfulness about what will happen. It is the fear of an unknown journey. But once you have been there and come out the other side, that fearfulness passes and something much more beautiful follows.

Rachel, who was 12, was such a good teacher about the unknown journey. She wanted to die in her own bed and not in hospital, where people did things to you. Four or five days before she died she became very peaceful and accepting. Reassuring her mother and me that it was going to be all right. And we needed that reassurance from her.

My dream is that our services will cover the whole of Britain, so that every family that has a child with a life threatening illness will be near enough for us to help if that is what they want.'

Extract from The Sunday Times Magazine
'A Life in the day of Bernadette Cleary'
- founder of Rainbow Trust.

~ ❖ ~

Index Of First Lines